The Panic Attack

THE PANIC ATTACK

Table Of Contents

Foreword

Panic attacks are dangerous but they are almost harmless from physical point of view. They are a type of anxiety which can reach its optimal level. These attacks are found in almost whole world but U.S is a big victim of these attacks and according to a research 20 percent of U.S citizens experience panic attacks at some point in their lives. This 20 percent means that, more than 50 million people will suffer from these panic attacks. About 2 percent of these people will go through a full extreme panic attack in which they may become totally psycho or mad. Normally first panic attack is experienced by people in their childhood or in teenage and usual range of age is 15-19.

Panic attacks or any other anxiety disorder is not developed suddenly instead there is a long history of the patient and gradually he becomes addicted to some fear. For example if someone has gone through panic attack while driving then, he will develop a fear or phobia of driving and he will start avoiding the situation. The point will come when the fear will become so high that he will not even go close to cars. This extreme situation may never come but if you did not do anything about that developed fear in start then, it will eat you out without warning.

The symptoms of panic attacks in children are different from symptoms of adults and other age groups because in children these attacks disturb their brain system mostly and they tend to damage their thinking power. Sudden decrease in school grades, sudden lost interest in certain sports or other similar symptoms are first symptoms of panic attacks and when you observe these symptoms then you should talk with the kid and get that fear out of his mind. In this EBook, I will try to guide you for the whole process of getting rid of these panic attacks.

There are hundreds of methods and techniques available and most of them involve therapies and very less medication is used to cure panic attacks. This is not because there is no medication made for this disease or disorder but medicines are just not as effective and they also possess side effects because normally when someone experiences this disorder then, he or she is not unfit physically and in a proper physical state if you start taking medicines then, those medicines will give you just side effects.

The Panic Panacea

Relieve Panic Problems From Even The Most Stressful Situation

Chapter 1:
Introduction to Panic Attacks

Synopsis

In this chapter, you will know the detailed description of panic attacks and will get to know the exact state in which they can occur.

❖ Initiating the cure

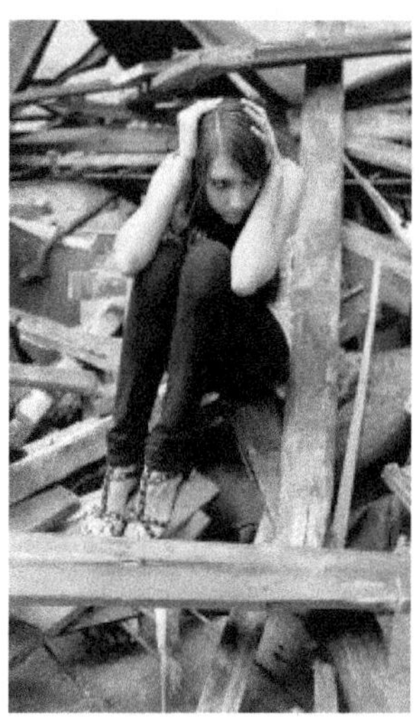

How To Start

Some dreadful feeling which causes extreme mental disturbance and psychological disorders in a person can lead to anxiety and panic attacks. You can categorize panic as a type of anxiety but this is more severe type of anxiety in which you can totally lose control of yourself and you become feared by some object, situation or any other event.

There is solution to these panic attacks but to explore those solution options, the sufferer bust explore the symptoms in the first place and need to know the triggering point of these attacks.

Some of the general symptoms for panic attacks are palpitations, nausea, trouble breathing, hyperventilation, trembling, and hot and cold flashes. The person who goes through these panic attacks often feels like he is going crazy and if some physical problem like chest pain or fatigue accompanies these attacks then, situation becomes even worse.

In general types, panic attacks will not last for more than 30 minutes but the duration can vary according to nature of panic attack and person's mental and psychological state.

Whatever your circumstances and situation is but you need to find a solution of these panic attacks as soon as you know about them because if you do not pay attention towards these attacks then, they can persist and can give you a long term physical or mental illness.

There can be different types panic attacks which all depend upon the type of anxiety you have but in more generalized way anxiety is categorized as obsessive-compulsive disorder, generalized anxiety disorder, phobia, post-traumatic stress disorder, panic disorder and social anxiety disorder.

Initiating the Cure

If you are experiencing some kind of panic attacks then, you must start a solution as soon as possible because if you delay the cure then, situation will become more and more dangerous and worse with every passing day. Everything starts from physical checkup and tests and when everything seems fine then, you need to consult some good psychologist to help you in this case.

He will know the symptoms and feelings which you can go through while experiencing panic attacks. Proper and healthy diet introduction can lead to less panic attacks and sleep is another very effective tool to help you in panic situations. People often suffer from sleeping disorder as a first symptom of panic attacks and if you are also going through this disorder then make it to go away as soon as possible.

There are so many other techniques available to control panic attacks and these techniques include distraction techniques, deep breathing techniques, muscle relaxation exercises and lot others and all of these techniques can help to reduce the frequency of these panic attacks and if you act on them regularly then you can even get rid of panic attacks completely.

In rest of the EBook I will tell you about these techniques in detail because most of the people are shy and they do not tell about these kinds of problems and seek information and cure help at their own.

This can be a wrong approach but you should keep looking for a solution whether you do it at your own or from your doctor. In this Book I will not tell you any medicine because taking or giving medicine without prescription of doctor is not legal and it can get you and me both in trouble. I will concentrate only on other methods which do not involve any medication

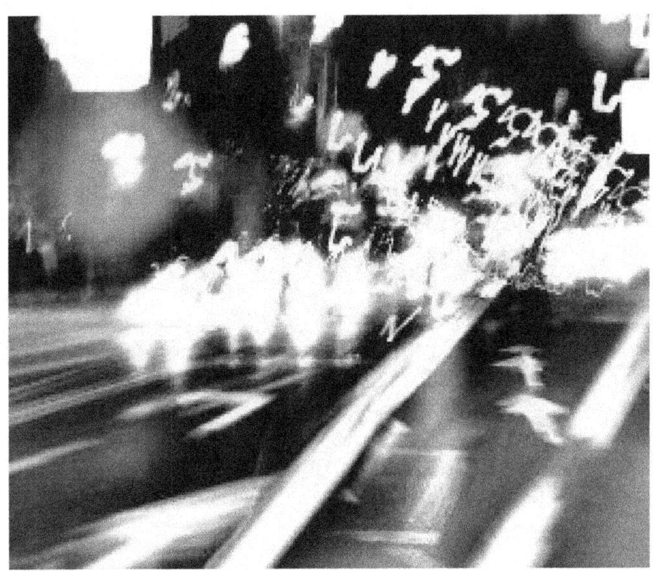

Chapter 2:
Symptoms of Panic Attacks

Synopsis

In this chapter I will tell you about detailed symptoms of panic attacks and will tell you all the triggering points which you can identify and control panic attacks.

❖ Breath inconsistencies

❖ Uncomfortable body sensations

❖ Catastrophic thoughts

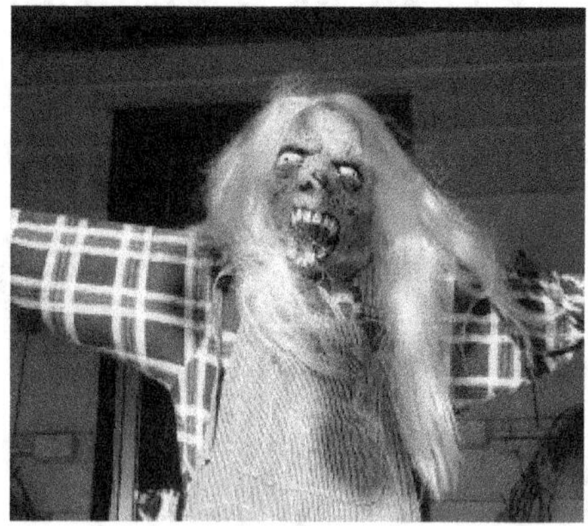

Symptoms

Most of the people think that panic attacks occur so suddenly that they cannot recognize their severances as well as any of their symptoms. This is true to some extent because mostly panic attacks occur without any prior warning but there are some prior symptoms which can always tell you about your state of mind and also some symptoms are such which can demonstrate the right way of reacting to these panic attacks and in this discussion, I am going to tell you about those symptoms.

Breath Inconsistency

First and most obvious symptoms of panic attack can be breathing disorder. A panic attack is nothing more than an emergency alarm of your body which is set to on by your rain. When you observe your breathing then, you will know that there are two things involved in breathing which are brain and lungs. You will hear a lot about air sacs, diaphragm and other similar parts of breathing system but the most important thing is central respiratory control system which is controlled by brain. Your brain is constantly observing the ratio of oxygen and carbon dioxide.

If the ratio of oxygen and carbon dioxide goes upside down then, your brain will trigger the emergency alarm. It may happen that brain tries to control this disorder in some way but if he does not succeed then, triggering the panic attack will be the only way. So if you keep an eye on your breathing system, you can tell that you are undergoing a panic attack.

Uncomfortable Body Sensations

Other than uncomfortable breathing, you can also have some prior body sensations which can tell you that you are about to have a panic attack. These body sensations can include Palpitations, pounding heart, or accelerated heart rate, chest pain and others. All of these will occur without a reason and you may sweat without hot weather.

You can feel numbness in some parts of your body and similar other gestures. All of these are controlled by brain and when you experience troubles then, you should know that brain has gone onto emergency plan and everything is becoming faulty.

Another very important and noticeable body sensation is less sleep because people who suffer through panic attacks often start to have less sleep which is also an important factor for determining the mental state of that person. Sleep has direct connection with your brain and without a peaceful brain you can never have a sound sleep. People often suffer through insomnia while suffering from panic attacks and they suffer severe kind of sleeping disorder.

Catastrophic Thoughts

These thoughts can come in your mind at any time and you will think like I am close to dying or I am losing my mind and similar other thoughts. These thoughts are so dangerous and powerful that they can make a person to commit suicide. You need to analyze yourself completely regularly and make sure that you are not experiencing these thoughts at all because if you are experiencing them then, you should look for a way to control them as soon as possible.

These are very general symptoms of panic attacks and you can identify them within yourself. It may be difficult at times to identify them and especially identify them before time but with some increased concentration and mind control you can successfully do that and once you start identifying the symptoms then, the rest of the procedure becomes easy and that is to cure these symptoms.

In rest of the EBook you will learn different techniques to control these symptoms and get rid of all kinds of panic attacks.

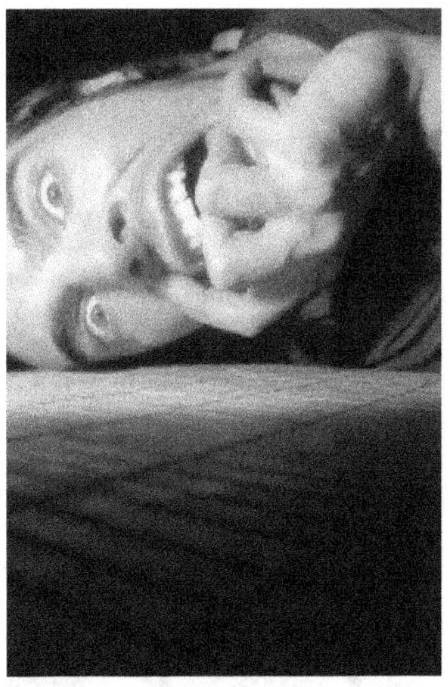

Chapter 3:
Types of Panic Attacks

Synopsis

In this chapter, I will guide you for all the possible types of panic attacks.

- ❖ Cued panic attacks

- ❖ Situational panic attacks

- ❖ Spontaneous panic attacks

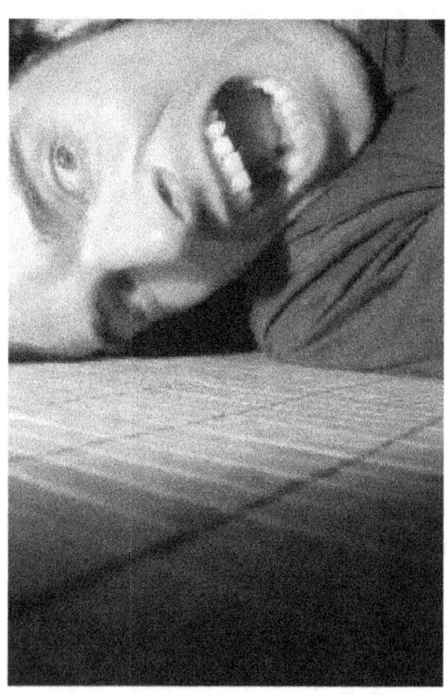

Sorts

Panic attacks can occur to anyone and at any time. They have different symptoms and sometimes they are correlated with some other physical and mental state of mind. It can be related to any phobia, anxiety, mental stress and other similar things and these panic attacks have different types which I am going to discuss in this chapter.

Cued Panic Attacks

Some people have panic attacks only in certain situations because they have a certain trigger point of their attacks and when that trigger happens, they experience panic. This kind of panic attacks are called cued panic attacks because in normal condition, these people remain normal and they act exactly same as other normal people but as soon as they face that typical situation then, they go through panic.

For example, if someone is not comfortable with social gatherings and he gets invited by someone then, he may go their but even if a single thing goes wrong in that gathering then, that person will feel lot more uncomfortable and will definitely lose patience and will be a victim of panic attack.

Situational Panic Attacks

Situational panic attacks are also associated with a certain event or place but people with situational panic attacks will not always experience panic attacks in that situation instead their response to same situation will be different. For example, if a person has a phobia or airplane ride then, he may experience panic attacks once going alone and he may not experience that panic attack with his family or friends.

So situational panic attacks are easy to cure because person already has tendency to react and control that attack. Such people just need very little anticipation to make it happen and control that situation.

Spontaneous Panic Attacks

This is most dangerous type of panic attacks because these attacks can happen at any time, anywhere and without any warning. The worst thing about these attacks is that they are not associated with ant triggering situation and they do not have any specific event or place to occur instead they are totally spontaneous and these are also the worst attacks to cure because their reason is unknown.

Chapter 4:
Diagnosing Panic Attacks

Synopsis

In this chapter, I will tell you the exact symptoms and methods which can help you to diagnose panic attacks effectively.

- ❖ Increased heart rate and abrupt breathing
- ❖ Chest pain and discomfort
- ❖ Numbness, dizziness and getting faint
- ❖ Trembling, shaking of hands and sweating even in normal weather
- ❖ Limited symptoms attack

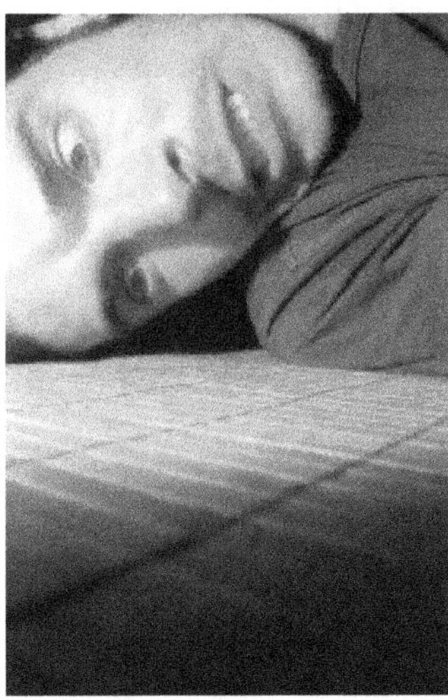

Getting It Handled

Panic attacks can be a cause for many mental and in some cases physical illness. Doctors who are treating any patient with panic attacks should always think of worst because panic attacks can be a very devastating disease.

Different people have its different forms and in every form it is more devastating than the other. People often confuse panic attacks with other mental illness but this should not happen and you should always know what you are dealing with.

There are very concrete methods of diagnosing panic attacks which you can implement and know that person is suffering through panic attacks.

Increased Heart Rate and Abrupt Breathing

If a person experiences an increased heart rate and an unusual change in its breathing then, he is certainly going through a panic attack because there are very few cases in which these symptoms appear and most of these cases lead to discovery of a panic attack.

Chest Pain and Discomfort

Person who goes through panic attack will also experience severe kind of chest pain and discomfort even in most comfortable position. for example if a person is resting in his bed room and talking on the phone, he can experience sudden chest pain, increased breathing and will feel very conscious then, you should know that he is going through a panic attack.

Numbness, Dizziness and Getting Faint

In extreme condition of panic attack, patient can also feel numbness in different parts of body and especially in hands and feet. He can feel dizzy and become faint but these symptoms appear very late and before these symptoms, you should get the patient some help because these symptoms are very acute and they can do a permanent physical or mental damage.

Trembling, Shaking Of Hands and Sweating Even In Normal Weather

Panic attack can cause the hands of the patient to vibrate ad shake very vigorously, he can sweat even in cold weather. These are very basic symptoms known for panic attacks and as soon as you observe these symptoms, you should call for some medical help because after these symptoms, some severe things will start to happen and they can give permanent damage to person's health.

Limited Symptom Attack

This is not necessary for every panic disorder patient to go through above symptoms instead he can go through a limited symptom attack also. This is a special kind of panic attack in which minimum symptoms appear which become very difficult to observe but person goes through a very severe kind of panic attack.

These attacks are even more dangerous because they can occur without much of alarming system. For example, a person can just experience an increased heart rate which is almost impossible to observe and with only one symptom, the person will go in severe condition of panic attack.

To avoid panic attacks, you just need to make sure that negative thoughts are not capturing your mind and even if you have some problem or tension then, share it with your friends and family members that can be really relieving.

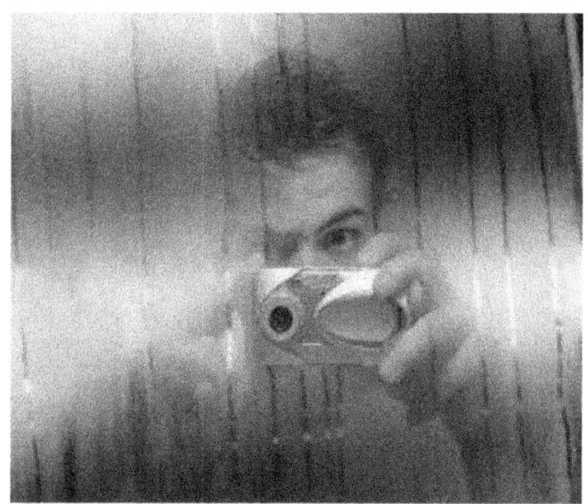

Chapter 5:
Importance of Medication in Panic Attack Treatment

Synopsis

In this chapter I will tell you about proper medication and importance of this medication during any panic attack or panic disorder.

- ❖ Panic disorder has no medicine

- ❖ Panic disorder is not a physical illness

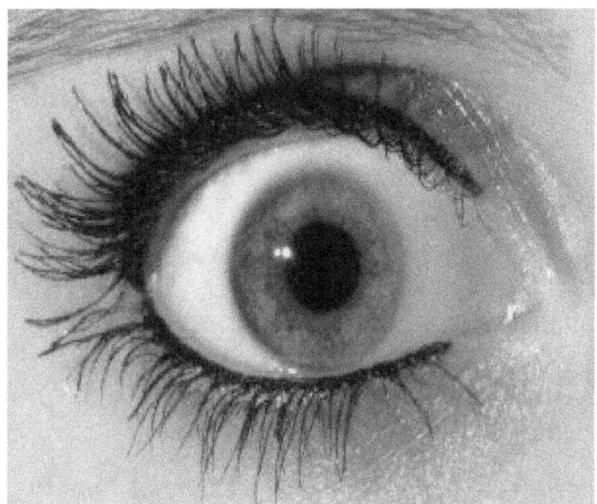

Medicine

Panic disorder is more relevant to mental disorder and there is very less medication available for this problem but doctors have done a very intense and thorough research on this subject and found some very effective medications. These medications may not be a full cure for your panic disorder but they do treat you up to 70 percent and rest is done through other treatment methods like different kinds of therapies and similar activities.

Panic Disorder Has No Medicine

Normally it is said that panic attacks cannot be treated with medicines and it is true to some extant because the core disorder of panic cannot be cured with medicines but its symptoms can be controlled with this medication easily. These symptoms and you can also call them effects of panic disorder like fast breathing, sweating, headache and other similar problems can be well-controlled with medicines. Normally doctors prescribe anti-depressant medicines to panic disorder patients because these medicines are made to relieve the mind and they give a sense of extra relaxation to patient's mind. He forgets about the tension and that situation in which he or she goes in panic state.

You can say that panic attacks are acute anxiety and when anxiety reaches to its worst state then, it becomes panic and it remains in that way unless or until you find a solution to this problem. You should never ignore the signs of panic attacks and do something about them as soon as possible.

Panic Disorder Is Not a Physical Illness

You need to know that panic disorder is not a physical illness instead it is just a mental response to certain tense and awkward situations. When your mind faces some uncertain and unbelievable event then, he responds in a very reluctant way and this reluctant way sometimes causes some confusion.

This is the reason that most of the therapists and physicians believe that this kind of mental illness cannot be completely cured with medication and in fact there is no proper medication available for this purpose. All the medicines which are prescribed are for temporary control and for mental relief. Therapies like cognitive behavior therapy and relaxation therapies are more widely used for treatment of panic disorder.

Chapter 6:
Cognitive Therapy

Synopsis

In this chapter you will come to know a very effective method to treat panic disorder completely.

- ❖ Cognitive behavior therapy depends upon emotional response
- ❖ What is CBT
- ❖ Improving behaviors
- ❖ Relationship between patient and therapist
- ❖ Goal setting
- ❖ Start focusing on present
- ❖ CBT is structured

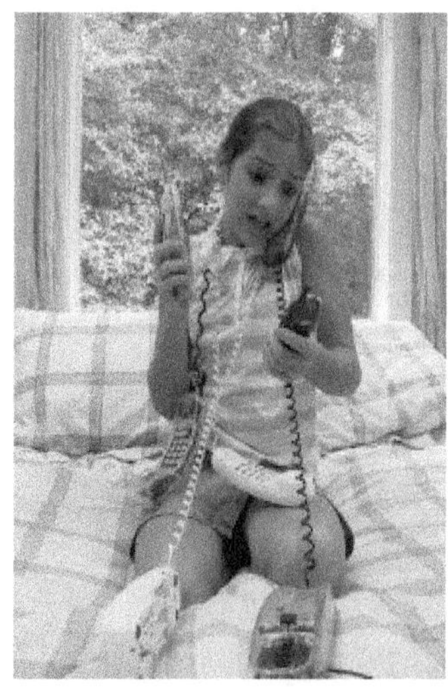

One Therapy

Cognitive behavior therapy is a types of psychotherapy which emphasis on the role of thinking and its impacts. It tries to get thoughts clean and helps the patients to overcome their negative thoughts. Cognitive behavior therapy is a more general term which includes some other therapies in it too and it consists of parts.

There are different techniques as Rational Emotive Behavior Therapy, Rational Behavior Therapy, Rational Living Therapy, Cognitive Therapy, and Dialectic Behavior Therapy. All of these therapies are included in the general type of cognitive behavior therapy.

Cognitive Behavior Therapy Depends Upon Emotional Response

In this therapy, it is not considered that our actions occur due to our surrounding physical factors instead in cognitive behavior therapy it is believed that our actions are caused due to our thoughts and our thoughts can impact on our overall behavior. The beauty of this therapy is that by changing our thoughts, we can change our surroundings and actions.

Cognitive behavior therapy is not only effective against panic disorder but it is also used in many mental diseases and its results are very satisfactory. Long researches have been carried out about this subject and lots of literature is published about this subject but people are still unaware about the full effectiveness of this therapy. Over last few years the popularity of cognitive behavior therapy has gained popularity and there are different reasons for this popularity.

First of all, in past few decades, there has been a gradual increase in mental and psychological problems, and CBT has proved a very decent way and effective against these mental and psychological disorders. There is a very structured, planned and in most of the cases very effective approach towards these problems. Another very important thing which is increasing the popularity of CBT is no medication involved and people prefer those methods of treatment which do not involve heavy medication.

What is CBT?

Cognitive behavior therapy is a type of psychological treatment which works by finding the correlation between our thoughts, feelings and actions. There is a time limited for this whole therapy to complete and normally this time period is less than a 2-3 months and it includes 10-15 sessions.

CBT is also known as family of mental treatments because different approaches are mixed and are implemented in a more collective and effective manner. CBT is known to be effective for people who have been undergoing other treatment as well or they have tried other treatments and have failed to cure.

You can also say that CBT is a process in which people are trained to think positive and their negative thoughts are eliminated. Thinking has a very deep effect on our daily life and multiple people seeing same event can interpret that event in different ways. For example if a glass of water is half filled then, some people will say that glass is half empty which is a discouraging thought while others can say glass is half filled which changes the whole approach.

Similarly, a person who is suffering from a panic attack may remember the gestures of a person who discouraged him but he will never remember the gestures of a person who appreciates him. These negative thinking adds more pressure and makes the situation tenser and sever.

CBT is the process to control these negative thoughts and bring the positive thoughts in front. In short, you can say that CBT tells you to control your thought which allows your mind to think more positively and more energetically. All of these things, if properly implemented, Can result in temporary or sometime permanent relief to panic disorder.

Improving Behaviors

Our thoughts affect our behavior and things which we think, we often execute and those things become our behavior and this behavior is needed to be changed which is done in CBT. A person who is going through a panic disorder is often facing lot more increases tension than a person who has forethought about that situation and adjusted according to the condition. This is the key thing which is to make adjustment according to your surroundings.

Parts of Therapy

The core therapy consists of different parts which are needed to be executed very precisely and accurately.

Relationship between Patient and Therapist

In order to make CBT more effective, practitioner of CBT which is an expert in his filed and patient, who is expert of his life, should cooperate and understand each other thoroughly. When a friendly environment is created and patient starts to share everything then, the problems begin to vanish and results start to come.

Goal Setting

Once the problem has been identified then, it is necessary for the practitioner to set a goal that how many sessions or how much time will be consumed to get that person again on track. This is important because as I mentioned above that CBT is always a limited time treatment.

Start Focusing on Present

This is obvious that you can never change your past but by thinking less about past, we can definitely make our present little better. Encouraging thought can make your future better because when you think less about your distressed past then, you feel new hope and strength to move ahead but if you keep thinking about the negatives of past then, it will become really hard for you to move on. It does not mean that you should totally forget your past instead you just need to remember past as a learning lesson and do not over pose your past in your present.

For example, if a person had a panic attack while addressing in public then, he will definitely feel very distress while going and addressing in public again but you need to make sure that you do not allow that past fear to overcome your mind. Start thinking it as a new day and try new things.

A CBT therapist will do the same and he will talk into the fears of patient and will change the perception of the patient about that particular event. Person experiences different beliefs and his whole perception of panicking from that situation changes.

CBT is Structured

As I mentioned above that time for CBT is predetermined and normally it is determined after first session. One session is not more than one hour in length. A qualified practitioner always sets up an agenda before every session which decides that which topics he is going to cover in a particular session and this agenda depends upon the problem of patient.

In fact, the between-session practice is also preplanned and patient is made to believe in treatment and he is encouraged and made ready to be cured. This kind of structured approach is beneficial and it produces very defined, concrete and fast results.

The Formulation of Treatment

By gathering all the data about patients, CBT practitioner makes a very fixed plan of treatment and this plan is normally made after a long research which includes the logs from hundreds of patients and their behavioral and physical gestures.

This is also an effective technique because lots of people can have similar problem and if you start keeping track of patients then, you can find an easy solution to certain common problems.

For example, if a person is going through panic attacks then, it is for sure that he has some trigger point which makes him afraid and he goes through panic. In order to make him normal, you need to make sure that he becomes so strong mentally that he faces his fear and once he faced his fear and realized that it was just a thought in his mind then, he will start taking that triggering point normal.

Chapter 7:
Relaxation Therapies for Panic Control

Synopsis

In this chapter, I will try to tell you some very effective and largely implemented relaxation techniques which can treat your panic disorder.

- ❖ Quick relaxation
- ❖ Process of long term relaxation
- ❖ Meditate your thoughts
- ❖ Your surrounding environment matters

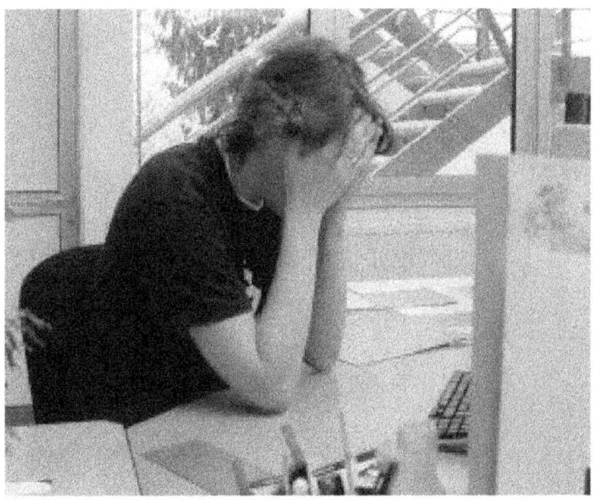

Relax

Relaxation techniques are a known method to treat panic disorder and these techniques are being used throughout the world. People have different opinions about these techniques but now days, as depression and mental disorders have increased, people have started to trust these techniques as an effective method to heal and help people in their mental disorders. In this discussion, I will discuss some of the known relaxation techniques which can help you in controlling your panic attacks.

Quick Relaxation

There are some exercises which can work wonders for you. For example if you just get some lose cloths and get comfortable, it sends a very soothing signal to mind. Get your toe muscles tight and hold them in tight position for 10 seconds then, release them and you will experience a great sense of relaxation in your whole body.

You can do this with all the other muscles of your body too because getting muscles in tension and then releasing that tension feels very relaxing and soothing for your whole body. Deep and slow breathing during this muscle relaxation is also helpful.

Process of Long Term Relaxation

The above mentioned exercises are just for short term relief and relaxation but when it comes to relaxing your mind then, you always need some strong relaxation techniques. People use relaxation techniques to get out of panic situation but those relaxation techniques need lots of practice to be learned properly. Now I will tell you some of those techniques in this discussion.

Meditate Your Thoughts

When people hear the word meditation then, they normally think that it will include some long and tiring exercise in which they have to sit and practice some unique exercise. This is not the proper mediation instead according to a certified physician the definition of meditation is stated as

"Any repetitive action can be source of meditation"

From this definition, it is evident that all the techniques like swimming, painting knitting and others can be a source of meditation for a particular person. In more brief way, you can say that any action which can keep your mind and thoughts in present is taken as meditation.

Your Surrounding Environment Matters

The environment in which you live has a very important role to play in making your thoughts positive and negative. Consciously, you cannot realize the difference between environments but you must have observed that it is easier to relax in certain parts of the house for example you may feel more relaxed in TV lounge than in your bedroom.

This can happen and you need to find that perfect corner of your house to relax where your body and mind can synchronize effectively. If you feel comfortable in certain set of accessories then, you should equip your bed room with those and make sure that when you relax then, it is 100 percent relaxing and your mind is not distracted anywhere.

Productivity Not Procrastination

This is another important thing to know that relaxation does not mean that you should become unproductive and spend your whole day sitting on your sofa and watching TV because this will make you dizzier and your mind will start to go into a different state.

Relaxation is about finding time to relax your mind during the usual activities throughout the day. Relaxing allows you to work with greater concentration and keeps your mind fresh.

Wrapping up

Panic attack is a psychological disorder which can be treated only with proper attention and proper therapies. There is not much medication available for this disorder. You can take some relaxing medicines to calm your brain but that will give you just temporary relief. The core problems lie in your thoughts and you just need to purify them, in order to make these panic attacks go. Panic attacks can range from minor mental disorder to long term physical illness. These attacks are needed to be controlled at a very early stage because as I mentioned that this is just a mental illness and once you let this mental thinking reside in your mind then, it becomes concrete and becomes very difficult to erase or modify them.

If you closely read this whole EBook then, you will come to know that you can cure this illness very effectively. Here are so many methods available which include both mental and physical exercises. I am 90 percent sure that everyone with basic knowledge of panic attacks, can cure it completely after reading this book an implementing all of the above mentioned techniques. There is no doubt about the fact that these techniques are hard to implement and you will need lots of concentration and struggle but once you get the main idea then, the rest of the process becomes easy.

Most of these methods are approved and tested with 100 percent success rate. The result and effectiveness of method depends upon the quality of practitioner because more qualified and experienced the practitioner is, more knowledge he will possess about the problems which are faced during the process.